pocket
cornwall

GW00643498

Birds of Cornwall
and the Isles of Scilly

David Chapman

Alison Hodge

First published in 2008 by
Alison Hodge, 2 Clarence Place, Penzance,
Cornwall TR18 2QA, UK
www.alisonhodgepublishers.co.uk
info@alison-hodge.co.uk

Reprinted 2011

ISBN-13 978-0-906720-55-4

British Library Cataloguing-in-Publication Data
A catalogue record for this book is available from
the British Library.

Designed and originated by BDP – Book
Development & Production, Penzance, Cornwall

Printed in China

Title page: Starling roost, Marazion

Contents

Introduction

Cornwall and the Isles of Scilly are wonderful places for bird watching. We have a wide range of habitats, including moorland, heathland, woodland, sand dunes, lakes, rivers, estuaries, and a hugely varied coastline. We have species of bird that are not found anywhere else in England, such as the chough, and we have seabirds that are the envy of those bird watchers living in land-locked counties. Geographical position puts Cornwall and the Isles of Scilly at the forefront of all bird watchers' minds during spring and autumn when birds are migrating. The valleys of West Penwith and the Isles of Scilly are the centre of attention when birds from as far afield as Asia, the Mediterranean and America find their way, mistakenly, to our shores. In late summer and autumn bird watchers gaze out to sea in the hope of seeing one of the many rare seabirds that are blown close to our shores by strong westerly winds. In autumn and winter we play hosts to thousands of birds escaping the cold of the continent: waders, wildfowl and thrushes can be found aplenty, and it is difficult to beat the spectacle of the huge starling roost at Marazion Marsh.

All of this, plus the fact that we have some of the most dramatic scenery in the country, makes Cornwall and the Isles of Scilly one of the best places to enjoy watching birds.

David Chapman
2008

Godrevy, on the north coast of Cornwall – an excellent spot for seabirds and migrants

About this Book

There are many field guides to the birds found in Britain and Europe, but the wealth of unnecessary information contained within them can cause confusion for people just starting out in bird watching. I hope that *Birds of Cornwall and the Isles of Scilly* will be useful to beginners wishing to identify the birds they see in their gardens or on walks in the countryside; more experienced bird watchers wishing to learn a little more about where to find birds in Cornwall and the Isles of Scilly, and visitors looking for information about the birds that they are likely to see.

In this book I have targeted the birds that can be seen regularly in Cornwall and the islands. As well as illustrating all of the common birds, there are also photographs of many less numerous species, particularly where these are of special local interest, such as the chough. Where appropriate, and where space allows, there are photographs that will help to distinguish the male of a species from the female, and young from adult. Altogether 130 species of bird are illustrated, in more than 160 photographs. Within the species descriptions are tips on where, in Cornwall and the Isles of Scilly, to go to find the species, and a calendar which shows when to look (the months are coloured green, with those in a lighter shade indicating periods when the bird may occasionally be seen). Listed at the back of the book are all the species likely to be recorded annually in Cornwall and the Scillies, with an idea of where and when they might be encountered. This will help you to make better use of more extensive field guides as your experience grows. Also included is a gazetteer of the top spots for bird watching in Cornwall and the islands.

The arrangement of species within the book is based upon the widely used taxonomic ordering of species, but at the back of the book the index is listed alphabetically. I have restricted the use of technical terms within the book to make it as easily understandable as possible when out in the field trying to identify a bird.

The Species

Great Northern Diver
Gavia immer

The most easily seen diver in the county. It spends winter at sea, occasionally visiting harbours and lakes near the coast during storms. Carnsew Pool is particularly good for this species. All divers, in winter (above), have white bellies and throats with a dark back. The great northern diver is best recognized from the red-throated and black-throated divers by its larger size and angular forehead. About the same size as a cormorant.

Little Grebe
Tachybaptus ruficollis

A small, dark grebe with a fluffy white rump. In summer (above) it has a chestnut-red throat and creamy patch at the base of its bill; in winter it is paler brown on flanks and throat with a dark back. It dives to avoid danger and often seeks the safety of over-hanging trees around ponds and lakes. In winter it can be more obvious on larger lakes and estuaries. In spring it makes a distinctive bubbling trill call.

J	F	M	A	M	J	J	A	S	O	N	D

Great Crested Grebe
Podiceps cristatus

In spring and summer (above) this bird has a wonderful chestnut and dark brown plumage around its head. Has an unusual courtship display involving the passing of weeds to a partner. In winter it is white underneath and dark on its back. This is quite a long-necked bird when compared to a diver and is slightly smaller. It occasionally breeds in county: try Colliford or Tamar Lakes and Stithians. It is commoner in winter on lakes and estuaries.

J	F	M	A	M	J	J	A	S	O	N	D

Fulmar
Fulmarus glacialis

Has a beautiful soft white plumage on its body, and pale grey wings. When seen close to it has a dark eye and a nostril tube along the top of its bill. Its flight is distinctive as it only occasionally flaps, more often gliding on stiff, straight wings. Nests around the coast on cliffs in small colonies. Present all year. One of the best locations to watch them is on the headland at West Pentire.

Manx Shearwater
Puffinus puffinus

Breeds only on islands – most notably Annet, one of the Isles of Scilly, making its nest in burrows. Can be seen offshore particularly on summer evenings and during westerly gales in autumn. Flies with stiff, straight wings, low over the waves. Is black on top and white below, and seems to alternate in colour as it turns in flight. Can form large flocks on the water at dusk before returning to nest sites. Boat trips are arranged on the Scillies to witness this 'rafting'.

Gannet

Morus bassanus

Unmistakable large white seabird with black wing tips. At closer range its yellow head can be seen. Juveniles show varying amounts of brown on their wings and body. Plunge dives for fish by folding its wings behind its body and diving head first from a great height. Doesn't breed in Cornwall but can be seen fishing around the entire coast throughout the year, visiting from Grassholm in Pembrokeshire. Photo: adult.

J	F	M	A	M	J	J	A	S	O	N	D

Cormorant
Phalacrocorax carbo

A large, dark seabird characterized by its wing-drying stance. Adults have a white cheek patch, and individuals of the continental race show a white thigh patch and head in the breeding season. Juveniles are brown with a paler belly and face. Occurs around the coast and at inland waterways. When diving to catch fish it slips under the surface without any effort. Can be seen around the county but one of the best locations is Loe Pool. Photo: adult wing drying.

Shag
Phalacrocorax aristotelis

Similar appearance and behaviour to the cormorant but smaller. Plumage is glossier with a green sheen, and in breeding plumage has a crest. Juveniles brown. Its small head gives it a daintier appearance, and when diving it tends to jump to gain momentum to submerge. A strictly coastal species which favours a rocky coastline. Nests on cliffs and islands around the county. Photo: adult on nest.

J F M A M J J A S O N D   J F M A M J J A S O N D

Grey Heron
Ardea cinerea

Tall and long legged the grey heron cannot be confused with any other Cornish bird. It has a grey back, white belly with black flanks and a black crest. Juveniles lack the black flanks and crest. Herons nest in colonies, usually in trees except for the colony at Marazion which nest in the reedbed. One of the best places to watch herons at a heronry is from the car-park at Millpool, East Looe. Stalks patiently and slowly for fish and can be seen on all estuaries, lakes, rivers and coasts. Photo: adult.

Little Egret
Egretta garzetta

Unmistakable large white wading bird. Dark bill and legs but yellow feet and eye. In breeding plumage has long nape plumes. Similar in structure to the grey heron but smaller and much more active in pursuit of prey. Can be found on any estuary in the county but the Camel is probably the best. Also hunts on the coast in rock pools. Is a breeding bird, with numbers boosted by migrants in winter.

| J | F | M | A | M | J | J | A | S | O | N | D |

| J | F | M | A | M | J | J | A | S | O | N | D |

Mute Swan
Cygnus olor

Very familiar bird of lake, pond and estuary. Huge size and white plumage make this bird obvious. Males have large black knob above bill. Bill colour is orange and black. Juveniles are brown. In flight the mute swan is most impressive, the sound of air being forced through its feathers is notable. Best places for large groups are probably Drift Reservoir and the Camel Estuary. Photo: adult plumage.

Canada Goose
Branta canadensis

A large brown goose with white rump, black neck and distinctive white cheek patch. This is Britain's largest goose and Cornwall's only common species. Occurs on lakes, and grazes surrounding fields. Originally introduced into Britain from North America. It is increasingly common in Cornwall, with large groups being recorded at Colliford, Crowdy and Siblyback reservoirs in particular. Photo: adult.

Shelduck

Tadorna tadorna

A dabbling duck. This is our largest duck. It is boldly marked with brown breast-ring, dark green head and red bill on a body comprising of white, black and brown plumage. Juveniles are sooty and white with a pink bill. Breeds in woodlands bordering estuaries where it finds food by sifting through the mud. Numbers are boosted by migrants in winter and spring, but almost all leave the county during August and September when they go to Bridgwater Bay, in Somerset, to moult. Photo: adult male.

Wigeon

Anas penelope

A dabbling duck. Attractive, with dainty head profile and bill. Drake (top) has a yellow forehead and brick-red head. His grey flanks contrast with a black rump. The female (above) is rusty brown. Visits Cornwall in winter and can be found in huge numbers on estuaries, with Hayle the best location in county, closely followed by the Camel and St John's Lake.

J F M A M J J A S O N D

J F M A M J J A S O N D

Gadwall

Anas strepera

A dabbling duck. Males are grey with an obvious black rump. Females are brown all over, so they can look like female mallards but have a much daintier-shaped head. This species is never found in huge numbers in Cornwall but a few regularly over winter at lakes and estuaries including Marazion, Hayle, Loe Pool and Drift Reservoir. Photos: drake (top) and drake and duck.

Teal

Anas crecca

A dabbling duck. This is a very small duck. The drake (top) has a beautifully marked, brick-red and green head, and a cream-coloured rump. Females (above) resemble small female mallards. It can be found at any estuary or lake in Cornwall throughought the winter months.

J	F	M	A	M	J	J	A	S	O	N	D

J	F	M	A	M	J	J	A	S	O	N	D

Mallard

Anas platyrhynchos

A dabbling duck. A common resident duck found on all Cornish waterways, including occasionally the coast. Drakes have a green head, brown breast and grey body. Females are brown all over. As with all ducks mallards moult in late summer when they all become brown and difficult to identify. Photo: drake (in front) and duck.

Pintail

Anas acuta

A dabbling duck. The drake is very distinctive with his long, thin tail feathers, but his chocolate-brown head and white neck stripe are also noticeable. Females are brown but have an elegant shape with a long neck and body. Apart from the shelduck this is our largest duck. Only occurs in Cornwall in small numbers during the winter months, usually on reservoirs and lakes. Photo: drake (at back) and duck.

J	F	M	A	M	J	J	A	S	O	N	D

J	F	M	A	M	J	J	A	S	O	N	D

Shoveler

Anas clypeata

A dabbling duck, made obvious by its huge, shovel-shaped bill with which it sifts the water for food. Drakes (top) have a green head and obvious chestnut-coloured flanks against a white and black body. Ducks (above) are brown, but their bill shape makes identification easy. Small numbers visit the county in winter and are usually seen on reservoirs and lakes.

Pochard

Aythya ferina

A diving duck with large, rounded head shape. Drakes (above) are grey with a red head and black breast and rump. Females (top) are fairly drab brown, but with darker breast and tail and some whitish smudges on the cheeks. Likes deep water and is numerous on Loe Pool in particular but can be found on reservoirs around the county.

| J | F | M | A | M | J | J | A | S | O | N | D |

| J | F | M | A | M | J | J | A | S | O | N | D |

Tufted Duck
Aythya fuligula

A diving duck. Male (top) is black with white flanks, the black glossed with purple. He has a tuft of feathers behind his head. Female (above) is brown, with the vestiges of a tuft behind her head. She may have a small patch of white at the base of her bill, reminiscent of a female scaup, but the scaup has a larger white patch and much bigger, more rounded head. Found at lakes and reservoirs in winter.

Common Scoter
Melanitta nigra

A diving sea duck which is most frequently seen from headlands, but which sometimes visits reservoirs during storms. Drakes (left) are black all over except for a small amount of yellow on the bill above which is a knob. Females (right) are brown with a paler cheek patch. Doesn't breed in the county so is more numerous in winter, but some non-breeding birds occur in summer. A good pair of binoculars will be required to find one at sea from a headland.

| J | F | M | A | M | J | J | A | S | O | N | D |

| J | F | M | A | M | J | J | A | S | O | N | D |

Goldeneye

Bucephala clangula

A small diving duck with a rather stumpy appearance and relatively big head. Drakes (top) are largely white but with a glossy green head contrasting with a white cheek patch. Females (above) are grey-brown with a white neck and brown head. Both have golden eyes. Can be found on estuaries, lakes, reservoirs and around the coast during winter. Loe Pool and the Carrick Roads are good for them.

Red-breasted Merganser

Mergus serrator

A large diving duck with a slim profile, known as a sawbill because of the serrated edge to its bill which it uses to catch fish. The drake (top) has a green head with a scruffy patch of feathers forming a double crest. His body is white, black and brown, with a reddish-brown breast. The female (above) is grey-brown with a reddish-brown head and a similar crest. Their bills are long and very thin. Seen on estuaries and around the coast in winter, especially the Carrick Roads.

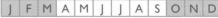

Goosander

Mergus merganser

A diving duck similar in size and shape to a merganser. The drake (left) has a green head but this is larger than the merganser. Unlike the merganser he has very clean, cream-coloured flanks. Females (right) are grey-brown with a white neck, strongly demarcated dark brown head and a white throat patch. The goosander doesn't have the scruffy crest of a merganser, but can show a bulge in the plumage at the back of the head. Overall the goosander is bigger and bulkier than the merganser and is more often found on inland waterways such as reservoirs and rivers, but is never numerous. Try the Tamar Lakes.

J F M A M J J A S O N D

Sparrowhawk

Accipiter nisus

Male (above) has slate-grey back and is rusty red underneath. Female has brown back with brown barring on white breast. Male is about the size of a kestrel, the female larger. Hunts around the edges of gardens and woodland, flying very quickly, often through trees, in pursuit of prey. Soars on thermals, but never hovers. In flight its wings are broader and shorter than a kestrel, and it has a long tail. Often flaps quickly then glides. Resident.

Buzzard

Buteo buteo

A very common bird of prey most often seen perched on telegraph poles by roadsides, or soaring on thermals when it makes a mewing call. This is a large brown bird with a variable amount of creamy white plumage on its belly. Can be seen anywhere in Cornwall but likes to use the thermals created by south-facing slopes. Will try to hover into a strong wind.

Kestrel
Falco tinnunculus

The only bird of prey that can truly hover. Male has dark spots on a brick-red back and cream underparts with a grey head and tail. Female is slightly less colourful, being brick-red to brown with heavier dark spotting all over. Hunts over rough ground by hovering so is common around the coast and around road verges. When in flight has a long tail and whippy, pointed wings.

Peregrine Falcon
Falco peregrinus

A large falcon, bigger than sparrowhawk or kestrel, with extremely chunky body, short tail and short, stout wings. Is dark grey above and white with dark streaks below. Has a distinctive black face mask. Flight is strong and direct. Males are smaller than females. Most often seen around the coast, and can often be heard calling: a loud 'kek-kek-kek'.

J	F	M	A	M	J	J	A	S	O	N	D

J	F	M	A	M	J	J	A	S	O	N	D

Red-legged Partridge
Alectoris rufa

A small, dumpy bird of farmland. The white cheeks and streaked flanks are its most obvious features. Partridges tend to stay hidden in rank vegetation or crops, but occasionally they wander across roads. Only present in Cornwall because of it being introduced for shooting. This species is more common than our native species, the grey partridge which has grey and brown plumage with a reddish face.

J F M A M J J A S O N D

Pheasant

Phasianus colchicus

The male pheasant (left) is unmistakable because of its size, colour and outlandish courtship behaviour. The colour of male birds varies somewhat, from the most common golden brown to quite dark or pale variants. The female (right) is better camouflaged and more reserved. Widespread across the county in farmland, gardens and woodland. Photo right: pheasant chick.

| J | F | M | A | M | J | J | A | S | O | N | D |

Water Rail
Rallus aquaticus

Usually found only in reedbeds during the winter, but because it migrates at night can sometimes be found in unusual places at dawn. The water rail is usually a very shy bird, and is much smaller than a moorhen. It has a red bill, grey belly and streaking down its flanks; along its back it is brown with dark streaks. It has a perky tail which shows white undertail coverts when seen from behind. Try Marazion or Swanpool.

Moorhen
Gallinula chloropus

A large, almost black bird of lakes and ponds. Has a bright red bill with a yellow tip, white flashes along its flanks and a perky tail with two white flashes underneath. Often encountered in or out of water, often nervous but can be tamed and will then come to food in places such as Tehidy Country Park.

| J | F | M | A | M | J | J | A | S | O | N | D |

| J | F | M | A | M | J | J | A | S | O | N | D |

Coot

Fulica atra

Slightly larger than a moorhen, the coot has pure black plumage but with a white bill and shield above the bill. Is common on open fresh water. It has an interesting range of behaviour when courting, showing a lot of aggression to opponents. Will graze and dive for food.

J F M A M J J A S O N D

Oystercatcher

Haematopus ostralegus

A large wading bird with black and white plumage. Its red bill, eye and legs are quite striking. Its plumage varies through the year in that during winter it develops a white chin stripe. Is quite vocal, particularly in spring, when it calls 'kuweek-kuweek', or a high-pitched 'kick-kick' warning call. Breeds around rocky coasts of both Cornwall and the Isles of Scilly, and in winter can be found mostly on estuaries. Photo: summer plumage.

J F M A M J J A S O N D

Avocet
Recurvirostra avosetta

A large, white wading bird with black pattern on wing and head. The avocet has a distinctive, up-turned bill which it uses for sifting through the surface of the water for food. A very graceful bird, particularly in flight. Only occurs in winter, and the only reliable site is on the Tamar near Cargreen.

Ringed Plover
Charadrius hiaticula

A very small, very well camouflaged, wader often seen on beaches. Has a sandy brown back, a white belly, with black rings around its neck and face. Its bill and legs are orange in summer (above) but brown in winter. Black plumage becomes browner in winter. Nests on beaches on the Isles of Scilly but not in Cornwall. Found commonly on beaches (sand and shingle) through the winter where it feeds well above the sea's edge.

| J | F | M | A | M | J | J | A | S | O | N | D |

| J | F | M | A | M | J | J | A | S | O | N | D |

Golden Plover
Pluvialis apricaria

A medium-sized wader. Only visits Cornwall out of the breeding season when it spends time on farmland and estuaries, usually in large flocks. Plumage is always golden brown above, but varies underneath from black in summer to brown with a white belly in winter (above). When seen in flight its armpits (known as axillaries) are white. Often makes a plaintive 'keeyou' call.

Grey Plover
Pluvialis squatarola

A medium-sized wader. Similar in stature to the golden plover, but a bit fuller bodied. It is found around the coasts of Cornwall in the winter, but never uses farmland. It is more likely to be encountered in small groups than the golden plover and is less colourful, being a cold grey. In flight it has quite obvious black armpits. The Camel Estuary is a good location for them. Photo: winter plumage.

J	F	M	A	M	J	J	A	S	O	N	D

J	F	M	A	M	J	J	A	S	O	N	D

Lapwing
Vanellus vanellus

A medium-sized wader. From a distance it can appear to be black and white, but the plumage on the back is actually iridescent green. Has a black head and crest. Small numbers breed in county, but it is present in large numbers only during the winter when it sometimes mixes with golden plover flocks on fields and/or estuaries. Distinctive flight (above) and 'pee-wit' call.

| J | F | M | A | M | J | J | A | S | O | N | D |

Sanderling
Calidris alba
A small wader. Similar in colour to a knot but much smaller and in better proportion. Often has a dark shoulder patch. Sanderling feed at the edge of the sea on sandy beaches, and are very active moving up and down the beach with the breaking waves. Can be found on any sandy beaches including those of the Isles of Scilly. Photo: winter plumage.

Knot
Calidris canutus
A small wader. Seen only out of the breeding season and in small numbers. In winter (above) the knot is white with a pale grey back. It has a black bill and eye, and is quite short legged with a dumpy appearance. Can be seen on any of our estuaries, usually mixed in with the slightly smaller dunlin.

| J | F | M | A | M | J | J | A | S | O | N | D |

| J | F | M | A | M | J | J | A | S | O | N | D |

Purple Sandpiper
Calidris maritima

A small, stout but dull, grey-brown wader found exclusively on rocky coasts in winter. Underneath it is slightly lighter, but its white belly is heavily smudged. Has orange legs and bill. Regularly returns to favoured winter sites, including the rocks of Godrevy Point.

Dunlin
Calidris alpina

A small wader, similar in size to a sanderling. The upperparts vary from streaked brown in summer to grey in winter (above). Has a black belly patch in summer but loses this, to be replaced by variable streaking on the breast and flanks in autumn and winter. The bill is slightly down-curved but looks a little bent. Has occasionally bred on Bodmin Moor, but only common on estuaries in winter.

J	F	M	A	M	J	J	A	S	O	N	D

J	F	M	A	M	J	J	A	S	O	N	D

Snipe
Gallinago gallinago

Supremely well camouflaged and often reluctant to fly. This bird has a very long, straight bill and cryptic brown plumage. When disturbed it takes off, flying erratically from side to side and making a squelching call. It breeds in small numbers on Bodmin Moor but is more numerous in winter on damp, marshy ground, usually around lakes.

Black-tailed Godwit
Limosa limosa

A large wader, not quite as big as a curlew, and with a long, straight bill. Of the two types seen in Cornwall during the winter the black-tailed godwit is more numerous. Has a black tail and white rump, with black and white stripes along its wings. It is found on estuaries and in creeks. (The less common bar-tailed godwit has a more streaked appearance and in flight shows a white V-shaped rump on an otherwise brown back; it is found on more open estuaries but rarely on enclosed creeks). Photo: winter plumage.

| J | F | M | A | M | J | J | A | S | O | N | D |

| J | F | M | A | M | J | J | A | S | O | N | D |

Whimbrel
Numenius phaeopus

Resembles a small curlew, basically brown and with a down-curved bill. Unlike the curlew this bird has obvious creamy stripes over the eye and along the crest of its head, and its bill is shorter and more steeply curved. In flight the whimbrel is best distinguished from the curlew by its call: listen for its 'qi-hi-hi' call. Certainly most numerous in April and May as it migrates north.

Curlew
Numenius arquata

A large, easily identified wader. Its all brown plumage and a long, down-curving bill are diagnostic. Its call is a wonderfully evocative bubbling 'cur-leee'. Breeds in small numbers on Bodmin Moor, but only common outside of the breeding season on estuaries.

| J | F | M | A | M | J | J | A | S | O | N | D |

Redshank

Tringa totanus

A medium-sized wader, smaller than a godwit but larger than a dunlin. Has bright red legs and bill which fade a little in winter (above). Plumage is brown with streaking, fading to grey in winter. Bill is of medium length and straight. In flight it has a white trailing edge to its wings and a white, V-shaped rump. The redshank is a noisy, alert bird. There is one confusion species for the redshank, and that is the spotted redshank, found in only small numbers around the county. The spotted redshank is larger, paler (in winter), has a longer, slimmer bill, and lacks the white trailing edge to the wing.

Greenshank

Tringa nebularia

Slightly larger than a redshank, the greenshank has grey-green legs. It is pure white underneath with variable grey or dark grey plumage on its back. Its bill is slightly longer than a redshank and shows a slight up-turn along its length. It can be found on estuaries and creeks. In flight has dark wings contrasting with a white V-shaped rump and white and black barred tail. Photo: winter plumage.

Common Sandpiper

Actitis hypoleucos

A small wader, similar size to a dunlin but a slightly slimmer, more elegant profile. White underneath with brown on its back and strongly demarcated brown collar. Its white breast runs up to a patch just in front of the wing when closed, which helps to distinguish it from some rarer species of sandpiper. Continually bobbing motion is eye-catching. Seen in the county during migration, on the margins of lakes, rivers and estuaries, may over-winter.

Turnstone

Arenaria interpres

Slightly larger than a dunlin, but also very chunky. Quite variable in plumage through the year and between sexes, but always a mixture of white, black, brown and brick-red. Short, stout bill is used to turn stones, so this species is found on rocky shores but also on harbour walls. Quite tame and approachable, try St Ives or Padstow. Photo: winter plumage.

| J | F | M | A | M | J | J | A | S | O | N | D |

| J | F | M | A | M | J | J | A | S | O | N | D |

Black-headed Gull

Larus ridibundus

A small gull. In summer (top right) has a black head, more correctly described as a dark, chocolate-brown face. In winter (left) this is lost and replaced by a black spot behind the eye. Legs and bill are dark red. Look for the distinctive white leading edges to the wings in flight (above), which help to distinguish this from some rarer species. Juveniles show a mixture of brown patches on wing and body, and have brown legs and bill. Not common in the summer, found on estuaries, lakes and on fields during the winter.

| J | F | M | A | M | J | J | A | S | O | N | D |

Common Gull
Larus canus

A medium-sized gull. This is not a common gull in Cornwall. It is of attractive proportions, and is slightly smaller than the herring gull. It is only usually seen in winter, when its head is streaked, otherwise its plumage is white with grey wings and black wing tips. Its legs and bill are yellow, but fade in winter. Can be seen feeding in fields, or congregating on estuaries and lakes. Photo: summer plumage.

Lesser Black-backed Gull
Larus fuscus

A large gull about the same size as a herring gull, but with much darker wings and yellow legs. Has the same red spot on the beak that is present in the herring gull. Juveniles take two years to mature from their brown plumage. Breeds in small numbers around the county – the largest colony is on Gugh (Isles of Scilly). Otherwise quite numerous in winter on estuaries, reservoirs and around harbours.

| J | F | M | A | M | J | J | A | S | O | N | D |

| J | F | M | A | M | J | J | A | S | O | N | D |

Herring Gull
Larus argentatus

The archetypal Cornish 'seagull'. Grey back, white underneath, with a red spot on its beak and pink legs. In winter it develops a streaked head. Its wing tips are black with some white spotting (typical of most gulls). Juveniles take two years to mature from their brown plumage. This is the species that has been trained to scavenge in our harbour towns and nests widely on houses. Photos: adult winter (above) and second winter plumage (left).

J F M A M J J A S O N D

Great Black-backed Gull

Larus marinus

The largest of our gulls with a very dark grey back (darker than the lesser black-backed) and huge bill. This gull has pink legs which help to distinguish it from the lesser black-backed gull. Juveniles take two years to mature from their brown plumage. Breeds in small numbers, but more common in winter. Can be found around our estuaries and reservoirs, but is most easily observed in harbour towns such as Newlyn where it can be relatively approachable. Photos: adult (above) and first winter plumage (right).

J F M A M J J A S O N D

Kittiwake

Rissa tridactyla

A small, nimble and graceful gull which nests on cliffs around the county but is seen only out to sea for the rest of the year. Has a very soft white plumage with grey wings which have almost pure black wing tips. Its bill is yellow, its eye and legs are black. Listen for its characteristic 'kittiwaaake' call from nest sites. Juveniles have a black 'W' pattern along their wings and black smudges on neck and tail. Photo: adult plumage.

| J | F | M | A | M | J | J | A | S | O | N | D |

Sandwich Tern

Sterna sandvicensis

A large tern with long, thin wings. Very noisy, making a 'keereck' call in flight. Its wings are pale grey, its body is white. It has a black cap, black legs and long, black bill which has a pale tip to it. Juveniles are streaked, and moulting birds have some white on their forehead. Plunge dives for fish. Seen only on migration, particularly in sheltered bays. Photo: summer plumage.

Common Tern

Sterna hirundo

Slightly smaller than the sandwich tern, this species has red bill (with dark tip) and legs. White underneath, pale grey above, and with a black crown. Dives for fish but not to any great depth. Juveniles have a smudgy crown. Only seen as a migrant in Cornwall, but nests on small islands around the Isles of Scilly. Photo: summer plumage.

J	F	M	A	M	J	J	A	S	O	N	D

J	F	M	A	M	J	J	A	S	O	N	D

Guillemot
Uria aalge
Of the auk family, the guillemot is dark brown above, white below, with dark head and bill, and white cheeks in winter. It nests on cliffs, rocky islands off the coast, and on the Scillies. Stands penguin-like, and dives for fish. Rare in winter, it may be washed up, oiled, or blown close to shore. Photo: summer plumage.

Razorbill
Alca torda
Similar in size and build to a guillemot, but even darker plumage on its back. Nests in similar places, but is more inclined to nest among boulders and in crevices rather than on simple cliff ledges. Dives to catch fish. It has a flattened bill with distinctive white markings across and along it. Similar plumage to guillemot in winter. Photos: summer plumage (top), winter plumage (below) .

| J | F | M | A | M | J | J | A | S | O | N | D |

| J | F | M | A | M | J | J | A | S | O | N | D |

Puffin

Fratercula arctica

Smaller and dumpier than the other auks. Has red legs and a distinctive and colourful bill which it uses to catch many sand-eels in one trip (above). Very narrow wings, like the other auks, which whir a little in flight but are very good when diving. Nests on only a couple of offshore islands in burrows, but can still be found in good numbers on Annet (Isles of Scilly). Visitors can see them by taking a boat trip from St Mary's — May and June are best. Photo (right): summer plumage.

Feral Pigeon/Rock Dove
Columba livia
The rock dove is the ancestor of the feral pigeon. Pure rock doves do not exist any more in Cornwall. The purer forms have a white rump, grey body with two black wing bars, and a pink and green suffusion around their necks. Feral pigeons are commonly seen in towns, whereas doves with a wilder pedigree will be seen around cliffs on the coast.

Wood Pigeon
Columba palumbus
Large pigeon of farm and wood. Mostly grey; rosy breast, white patches on neck and wings. Numerous all year; often huge numbers in autumn/winter. White elbow patches on wings help distinguish it from the stock dove, which is slightly smaller and less numerous.

Collared Dove

Streptopelia decaocto

A common garden bird. Much smaller and daintier than the wood pigeon. Its plumage is pale buff with a small black collar around the back of its neck. Attractive in flight when it flutters and glides while spreading its wings and tail. Quite a noisy bird, with a range of cooing sounds.

Cuckoo

Cuculus canorus

Has long, pointed wings, long tail, grey back and a barred breast. Can resemble a bird of prey in flight. Females are similar but grey-brown above. Juveniles are brown with heavy barring all over. Call of the male (above) is a clear 'cuckoo', but females have a bubbling call. Adults are only present in the county from late April to July – after that it is the juveniles that we see. Seen mostly on heaths and moors including the Isles of Scilly.

Barn Owl
Tyto alba

Probably a few hundred pairs of barn owls nest in the county. A ghostly white apparition in front of the car headlights is most likely to be a barn owl. Although it is white underneath, it is yellowish-brown above. A graceful bird in flight, best seen in summer late in the day as it hunts to feed its young. Usually silent but has a screeching call. Nests in barns and tree holes, or purpose-built nest boxes.

Tawny Owl
Strix aluco

An owl of woodland and garden. This bird is dark brown and is quite squat. In flight it has broad wings and very short tail. It nests in tree holes or purpose-made nest boxes. This is the owl that makes the characteristic 'tuwhit-tuwhoo' sound, though actually this is a male and female bird responding to each other. Rarely seen by day, but occasionally calls during daylight.

| J | F | M | A | M | J | J | A | S | O | N | D |

| J | F | M | A | M | J | J | A | S | O | N | D |

Swift

Apus apus

Essentially dark brown, the swift has a small pale patch around its throat. Easily recognized by its sickle-shaped profile in flight. Continually on the wing, it is never seen at rest, except on the nest which is usually made in the roof spaces of old buildings. Its distinctive call is a piercing scream. Often flies in large numbers and nests in colonies. Larger than a swallow. Photo: characteristic profile in flight

Kingfisher

Alcedo atthis

Our most vividly coloured bird, with orange breast and bright blue back. Lives along rivers but often winters on estuaries. Has a black beak, but females (above) distinguished by their orange lower mandible. Very fast in flight and easily missed, but has a loud, high-pitched 'seeee' call. Nests in holes in riverbanks, and often perches on vegetation overhanging the water. Chaffinch-sized.

J	F	M	A	M	J	J	A	S	O	N	D

J	F	M	A	M	J	J	A	S	O	N	D

Green Woodpecker

Picus viridis

A very large woodpecker which feeds on ants found on the ground, though can of course be seen on trees where it nests. Has a red head, green body and bright yellow rump, a feature which is obvious as it flies away. Its flight is undulating and its alarm call is a very loud laugh, often described as a 'yaffle'. Is found where there is a mix of mature trees and open grassland. Male (above) can be distinguished from female by the red spot in his black moustache.

J F M A M J J A S O N D

Great Spotted Woodpecker

Dendrocopos major

Basically a black and white woodpecker found in woods and gardens. Male has a red spot behind his head, juveniles have a red cap, and all have a red vent (the area under the tail). Will come to the peanut feeder. Very undulating flight and a loud 'chick-chick' alarm call. Listen for them drumming in early spring. The only confusion species is the lesser spotted woodpecker, which is quite rare in Cornwall and is tiny in comparison. Photos: female (left) and juvenile.

J	F	M	A	M	J	J	A	S	O	N	D

Skylark
Alauda arvensis

Renowned for its beautiful song, which it utters in flight as it hovers. Quite a drab brown bird, about the size of a house sparrow, but with an appealing crest and a speckled breast. Found around the coast and on farmland, but is at its greatest density on dunes such as Penhale and Upton Towans.

Sand Martin
Riparia riparia

Has brown wings and a white belly. The brown extends on to the underside only around its neck, where a neat collar is formed. Flies a bit like a swallow but has much shorter wings and a stumpy, forked tail. A summer migrant which returns earlier than most and spends much of its time hawking for insects over fresh water or around the coast. Nests in holes in sandbanks, often in coastal cliffs.

Swallow
Hirundo rustica

A very graceful bird with long tail streamers. Its plumage is gun-metal blue on the back and head, and is creamy white underneath. It has a chestnut-red face. Always nests inside buildings, usually barns, by making a mud cup against the rafters. Young birds lack the tail streamers. Frequently calls a cheerful 'chit chit'.

House Martin
Delichon urbica

Dark, almost black, on its back and white underneath. Has a stumpy tail and wings, like the sand martin, but has an obvious white rump; because of this feature, when in flight it can look like the pair of wings is detached from the tail. Nests in a cup-shaped nest with a small entrance hole situated under the eaves of houses.

Meadow Pipit
Anthus pratensis

Smaller than a skylark, with heavily streaked brown upperparts and a breast which looks a little like that of a thrush. White edges to tail obvious when it flies low. Breeds in Cornwall but its numbers are massively boosted in autumn and winter by migrants. Is found on any rough grassland or moorland, and in winter can be found anywhere, including beaches, which can lead to confusion with the rock pipit. One useful sign of a meadow pipit is an accumulation of spots in the centre of its breast. Distinctive 'tsip-tsip' flight call.

Rock Pipit
Anthus petrosus

Slightly larger than the superficially similar meadow pipit, this is a distinctly smudgy grey-brown bird, much duller in colour than the meadow pipit. The spots on its breast and flanks are sooty brown. Found mostly on rocky beaches. In spring it has a wonderful parachuting display flight.

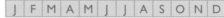

Grey Wagtail
Motacilla cinerea

Has a bright yellow rump which continually wags. The back of its wings and head are grey. Adult males have a black throat and subtle yellow belly, but females (above) and immatures have a whitish throat and only a yellow wash underneath. Lives along rivers and by lakes during the summer, but is more widespread in winter. Its close relative, the yellow wagtail, is found only rarely on migration in Cornwall, and has a green back.

Pied Wagtail
Motacilla alba yarellii

Familiar black and white bird of town and country. It is very variable in plumage between male, female and juvenile and there is a subspecies known as the white wagtail, but all are very distinctive with their long tail. Has a very familiar 'chizzick' call. Most numerous in winter when it forms roosts at favoured locations; there is one in Treliske Hospital, Truro.

J	F	M	A	M	J	J	A	S	O	N	D

J	F	M	A	M	J	J	A	S	O	N	D

Dipper
Cinclus cinclus
This is about the size of a thrush, but with the profile of a wren. It has a white breast, brown head and belly, and a black back. It often perches on rocks in the river where it bobs incessantly. Entirely associated with fast-flowing rivers, it nests under bridges and tree roots and catches insects under water. Good spots include the upper reaches of the River Camel, Golitha Falls and Kennall Vale.

Wren
Troglodytes troglodytes
A tiny, brown bird commonly found across Cornwall. Has a characteristic stance with erect tail. Surprisingly loud for a bird of its size, its song is long and cheerful and always ends in a trill. Makes a domed nest low down in vegetation, but sometimes adapts the nests of other birds such as swallows.

J	F	M	A	M	J	J	A	S	O	N	D

J	F	M	A	M	J	J	A	S	O	N	D

Robin

Erithacus rubecula

Its red breast makes this an easily identifiable bird. Has a brown back and creamy white belly, and some grey plumage around the side of its head. Young are brown and speckled. Very common in gardens. Lovely, clear song and a variety of other calls. Quite aggressive and territorial throughout the year, though birds will share food at a bird table (reluctantly!). Photos: adult (left) and juvenile plumages.

Dunnock

Prunella modularis

An unobtrusive bird which lives around hedgerows and gardens. It is rather drably coloured brown on top with a grey head, and it skulks at the bottom of hedges. Often referred to, inaccurately, as a hedge sparrow. Has quite an attractive song and often calls 'seeh' from the undergrowth. About the size of a robin.

Black Redstart
Phoenicurus ochruros

Females and juveniles, which make up most Cornish records of this species, are sooty brown all over, but with a flash of red at the base of the tail. Males also have the red flash in the tail, but have a black face and breast and are dark on the back with a white wing panel. A rare bird, but sometimes occurs in quite large numbers around Cornwall and particularly the Isles of Scilly during its autumnal migration. Often found feeding on insects around decaying seaweed on beaches. About the size of a robin. Photo: young male.

Redstart
Phoenicurus phoenicurus

The male (above) is a wonderful bird with black face, grey back and red breast and belly. The female is brown on the back with a reddish tinge to her underparts. Both sexes have a red flash at the base of the tail. Breeds in small numbers around Bodmin Moor and sometimes in Lanhydrock. About the size of a robin.

| J | F | M | A | M | J | J | A | S | O | N | D |

| J | F | M | A | M | J | J | A | S | O | N | D |

Stonechat

Saxicola torquata

The male (above) has a rosy red breast and dark back, with an almost black head and a white line on either side of his neck. Females and immature birds show some pink in their breasts with a brown head and back. Usually obvious because of their habit of perching on top of bushes to call. Have a pebble-tapping call, hence their name. Often seen around the coast, but also common on heathland.

Wheatear

Oenanthe oenanthe

Has a grey-back and white belly with a wash of orange on the breast. Males have a black line through the eye from the beak. Both male (above) and female (top) have darker wings and a black and white tail. About the size of a robin with a very upright stance. Hops along the ground quickly and perches on rocks or fence-posts. Often found around the coast on migration, and some birds stay to breed on the coast or Bodmin Moor.

| J | F | M | A | M | J | J | A | S | O | N | D |

| J | F | M | A | M | J | J | A | S | O | N | D |

Blackbird
Turdus merula

Male (left) is black with orange-yellow legs, eye-ring and bill (birds on Isles of Scilly have a much deeper orange bill). Females (above) are brown, with a slightly speckled throat and breast. Young males are dark but have a dark bill. Common throughout the year but even more numerous in winter

| J | F | M | A | M | J | J | A | S | O | N | D |

Song Thrush
Turdus philomelos

A small thrush with brown back and a cream breast and belly spotted with dark brown. Typically found in gardens feeding on the lawn or under the shrubs. Eats worms and snails – the latter are opened by hitting them against a stone anvil. In flight reveals a yellow-orange underwing. Song is distinctive as its fluty phrases are always repeated. Less common than it once was, though very common and tame on the Isles of Scilly.

J F M A M J J A S O N D

Fieldfare
Turdus pilaris

A large thrush, even bigger than a blackbird. Has a grey head and rump, reddish-brown back and heavily smudged and streaked breast and flanks. Has white underwings. Occurs in flocks around farm fields and hedgerows. Is usually noisy, making a loud 'chack-chack' call. Visits in winter and feeds on berries from hedges or larvae from short, grassy fields.

Mistle Thrush
Turdus viscivorus

Our largest thrush. Similar to a song thrush in plumage, but its colour always looks a colder and greyer brown. It has white underwings. Doesn't tend to come to gardens, it favours wider open spaces such as parkland habitat. Not usually found in flocks; never in such big flocks as the redwing and fieldfare. Has an undulating flight like a woodpecker, and often calls in flight. Its call sounds a little like a football rattle.

Redwing

Turdus iliacus

Our smallest thrush, the redwing has a dark brown back, and a white belly with dark spots. The face pattern, particularly its pale supercilium, is obvious from a distance. In flight it reveals a red underwing which extends on to its flanks. It occurs in flocks and is most obvious when feeding on berries in the late autumn, but it also feeds on short, grassy areas. Has a distinctive flight call which is a whispy 'tswooeep'.

Cetti's Warbler
Cettia cettia

A large warbler, about the size of a robin. This is a drab, brown bird, slightly paler underneath with a feint creamy supercilium. It is found exclusively around reedbeds. Though extremely shy and secretive, it draws attention to itself through its loud call which consists of an explosive series of notes. The best season to hear one is early spring; the best time is early morning, and the best place is Marazion, though other reedbeds such as Par Beach Pool also have them.

Sedge Warbler
Acrocephalus schoenobaenus

Streaky brown upperparts, pale underparts and a striking white supercilium make the sedge warbler conspicuous in its reedbed environment. Juveniles, in late summer, have a feint crown stripe which can lead to confusion with the aquatic warbler (but this has a well-defined crown stripe and is a very rare visitor, almost exclusively to Marazion and only in August and September). Often seen on top of reed stems singing. Song is similar to reed warbler but more varied.

J	F	M	A	M	J	J	A	S	O	N	D

J	F	M	A	M	J	J	A	S	O	N	D

Reed Warbler

Acrocephalus.scirpaceus

Its brown back and cream belly make this quite a plain-looking bird. Its head shape is unlike most warblers in that it is long, with a flat forehead and longish beak. Found exclusively around reedbeds. Its song is nasal and repetitive, consisting of 'trrrr', 'grrrr' and 'chrrr' notes.

Dartford Warbler

Sylvia undata

Dark grey above and wine-coloured below. Distinctive red eye and eye-ring. The male has a scratchy 'tchrrrare' call. Usually secretive but sometimes sings from gorse spikes in spring. A resident species of warbler which nests among gorse on heathland. Becoming more widespread across the county, Kit Hill is regarded as a stronghold.

Whitethroat
Sylvia communis

A large warbler. Both sexes have brown wings and creamy belly, male (above) has a grey head and white throat, whereas the females are mostly brown. Lives in hedgerows but is most numerous around the coast, often using gorse to nest in. When it returns from Africa in April and May it is very vocal and easy to see, after this it becomes more secretive. The male often sings in obvious places and his short, scratchy song draws attention.

Blackcap
Sylvia atricapilla

A large warbler with brownish-grey plumage, slightly darker on back than underneath. Males (above) have a black cap, females a brown cap. Usually a summer visitor, but a few over-winter in Cornwall and come to bird tables. In spring they have an attractive song with fluty phrases interspersed with chattery notes. Gives a harsh 'chack' warning call from heavily concealed places. (The garden warbler's song is similar but longer. The garden warbler is less common, has warmer brown plumage and no black head.).

Chiffchaff

Phylloscopus collybita

A small warbler whose plumage varies from buff to grey-green. It sometimes shows a small flash of yellow in the 'elbow'. Paler underneath than on top and with a feint supercilium. Can be confused with the willow warbler but is slightly daintier in appearance and almost always less colourful. Usually has dark, almost black, legs. Its song makes this bird instantly identifiable since it sings its name, 'chiff-chiff-chiff-chaff'. Breeds in the county, is very numerous on migration, and also occurs in small numbers during the winter.

Willow Warbler

Phylloscopus trochilus

Similar to the chiffchaff though slightly larger, with longer wings and a fuller body and head shape. Has a paler beak and legs than the chiffchaff. Juveniles are often quite yellow on breast and belly. The song of the willow warbler is one of great beauty. Its fluid notes start with a high and descend as the verse progresses, very much a reminder of spring.

Goldcrest
Regulus regulus

Our smallest bird, even smaller than the wren. Has a green-grey back and is slightly lighter underneath, but its most striking feature is its head pattern. It has a yellow flash along its head which is surrounded by black. The male's head streak is more orange. The similar firecest (which is rare) has an additional white supercilium, making it even more striking. Feeds by picking insects from branches, often in evergreens. A thin, whispy 'seeee-seeee' call which it uses regularly.

Pied Flycatcher
Ficedula hypoleuca

Slightly smaller than the spotted flycatcher, this bird is much more striking in appearance. The male (above) is black and white, the females and juveniles are sooty brown and white. Lives in oak woodlands and will nest in nest boxes. Sometimes breeds in the east of the county, but is more often seen on migration. The woods of Lanhydrock are a good place to try, so too are Cabilla and Redrice Woods.

Spotted Flycatcher

Muscicapa striata

A fairly plain-looking bird, about the size of a robin, with brown back, cream belly and feint streaking on its breast. It is the behaviour of this bird that makes it a wonder to watch. It usually perches on a favoured branch and makes airborne sallies to collect insects before returning to the same perch. Likes to nest in holes in old walls, often among climbers, and will use open-fronted nest boxes. Not common but uses traditional sites often around old houses and churches. Lanhydrock usually has one pair in the main garden around the house.

Long-tailed Tit

Aegithalos caudatus

Very distinctive bird with cotton-wool body and extremely long tail. Plumage pale underneath and dark on top with a pink suffusion throughout. Juveniles have chocolate-brown face markings rather than black. These birds gather together in flocks during winter, when they are at their most obvious, usually calling 'tsssirrrr' to each other as they progress along a hedge.

Marsh Tit

Parus palustris

Has a brown back, buff underparts, black cap (and chin) and white cheeks. Superficially like blackcap in appearance, but much smaller. Breeds in the county and is resident. Despite its name can be found in any woodland habitat. Listen for its loud 'pitchoo' call. The similar willow tit, which is much less common, has a larger head, bigger black bib and a pale wing panel.

Coal Tit

Parus ater

This bird has a creamy brown belly, grey wings, black head with white cheeks and a white nape patch. It lives in all types of woodland but is most common among evergreen trees. Will come to bird feeders and usually takes seeds away to store for later.

J	F	M	A	M	J	J	A	S	O	N	D

J	F	M	A	M	J	J	A	S	O	N	D

Blue Tit
Parus caeruleus
A strikingly colourful bird with blue wings and head, green back, blue legs and yellow breast. Has a feint line up the centre of its breast. Juveniles are similarly patterned but show less contrast in their plumage. Common in woodlands and gardens. Photos: adult (above) and juvenile plumage.

| J | F | M | A | M | J | J | A | S | O | N | D |

Great Tit
Parus major

A large tit with striking yellow belly, green back and black and white face markings. Has a black line up the centre of its breast which is broader in the male (above) than the female. Juveniles are similarly marked but show less contrast. Quite varied in its calls but has one distinctive phrase: 'teach-er, teach-er'. Common in woodlands and gardens and will come to feeders.

Nuthatch
Sitta europaea

Grey on top and pale brick-red underneath with a black eye-stripe. An acrobatic bird, capable of walking up and down tree trunks head first. Surprisingly small, no bigger than a great tit. In winter often mixes with tit flocks, in summer lives around mature trees where it makes its nest in holes. Found throughout Cornwall, but more common in the east, especially the Tamar Valley around Cotehele.

J	F	M	A	M	J	J	A	S	O	N	D

J	F	M	A	M	J	J	A	S	O	N	D

Treecreeper
Certhia familiaris

White below and a wonderfully well camouflaged pattern of brown and cream on its back. The treecreeper spends its life climbing up the trunks of trees in search of insects, often spiraling up to the very top before flying down to the base of the next one. Its stop-start technique is characteristic and almost mouse-like. On closer inspection the treecreeper has a fine down-curving bill with which it probes into cracks in the bark. It is not as common in Cornwall as it is in other counties because of the shortage of mature trees, so it is more frequent further east in the county.

J F M A M J J A S O N D

Jay

Garrulus glandarius

A large bird with a body about the same size as a magpie, to which it is related. The jay is very colourful, being mostly pink but with a blue flash in the wing, a bright white rump, black and white in the wings and tail, and a black moustache. The jay is shy but noisy, often making a raucous call if disturbed; when settled will make a gentle mewing sound a little like a buzzard. Found in deciduous woodland.

Magpie

Pica pica

Black and white plumage combined with a long tail make the magpie quite obvious. The black plumage is actually glossed with green, purple and blue if seen in good light. Lives in woodlands and will visit farmland and gardens to feed. Has a loud 'chack chack' call.

Chough

Pyrrhocorax pyrrhocorax

A small, glossy black crow with striking red legs and red, down-curving beak. Juveniles' beaks and legs are brown-red. Lives on the coast, feeding among short turf of coastal fringe and cattle pastures. Is recognizable in flight from a jackdaw by its broader wings and splayed finger tips. Has a very enthusiastic 'chiow-chiow' call, though its name is now pronounced 'chuff'. Breeds at only a small number of locations in Cornwall, and the best known site is near Lizard Point.

J F M A M J J A S O N D

Jackdaw

Corvus monedula

A small common crow with black plumage and a grey head. Its call is a 'chack' or sometimes a 'keeargh'. Can be found around the coast of Cornwall, and also around evergreen trees and old buildings. Sometimes forms large roosts in the winter. Feeds on short turf of the coast and on farmland. Sometimes associates with flocks of rooks.

Rook

Corvus frugilegus

A large black crow with a purplish tinge to its plumage. It has a whitish beak and a bushy plumage around its legs and rump. Juvenile birds, into their first winter, lack the white on the bill. Nests in large colonies, known as rookeries, high up in the trees. Often found in large flocks feeding on farm fields. Is quite vocal, with a range of metallic notes and sharp fragments as well as the more drawn-out 'craaaaa'.

| J | F | M | A | M | J | J | A | S | O | N | D |

| J | F | M | A | M | J | J | A | S | O | N | D |

Carrion Crow
Corvus corone

A large black crow with black legs and beak, confusable only with a juvenile rook and possibly a distant raven. The carrion crow is usually found singly or in small groups. Lives mostly inland, nesting in trees and feeding in farm fields. This is much smaller than the raven.

Raven
Corvus corax

A huge black crow with extremely thick neck and large black beak. Its plumage is tinged with purple. In flight the raven usually calls, and these sounds consist of deep honks and croaks. Also in flight the shape of its tail is often noticeable: this comes to a wedge-shape at the end rather than being straight across the tip. Also look for a long-necked profile in flight. Most frequently nests around the coast, but also in large evergreen trees. Often found in small family groups.

J	F	M	A	M	J	J	A	S	O	N	D

J	F	M	A	M	J	J	A	S	O	N	D

Starling
Sturnus vulgaris

A wonderful dark, almost black, glossy plumage mixed with purple and green tinges. The starling is speckled with white spots. Juveniles (above) are brown and moult from the bottom upwards so show varying degrees of adult plumage (left) in late summer. Gregarious, often flocking together, and form huge roosts in autumn and early winter. Marazion usually has one of the largest, but Crowdy Reservoir and Par Beach Pool are also good.

J F M A M J J A S O N D

House Sparrow
Passer domesticus

A charming bird w ith real character. The chestnut brown of the male's back contrasts with his grey body, brown tail and black bib (below left). Females (above) and juveniles are brown all over if a little paler underneath. Has a distinctive 'churp' call. Common in gardens and farm yards, nests in colonies in roof spaces and the like. Similar only to the tree sparrow, which is rare in Cornwall and which has a maroon cap and black spot on its white cheeks. Photo top right: female dust-bathing.

| J | F | M | A | M | J | J | A | S | O | N | D |

Chaffinch

Fringilla coelebs

A familiar bird of garden and woodland. The male (right) has a pink breast, grey head, green rump and black and white wings. The female (above) is buff underneath. Has a loud song consisting of an accelerating trill and a distinctive 'chink' call. Common throughout the year, usually occurring in flocks during the winter. Only confusable with the brambling which is a rare visitor to Cornwall in the winter. The brambling has orange tones in its breast, streaked plumage and a white rump.

J F M A M J J A S O N D

Greenfinch
Carduelis chloris

A large finch found commonly in woods and gardens. The male (above) is green with yellow flashes in its wings and tail. The female is browner, though still has the yellow flashes. Juveniles are similar to the females, but are streaked underneath. Can be quite aggressive at the bird table. Male has a lovely song flight in the spring, which consists of a fluttering parachuting display.

Goldfinch
Carduelis carduelis

A distinctive and colourful bird with red, black and white face, brown body, and black and white wings. Juveniles have a plain brown face. All have a flash of yellow in the wing. Feeds on small seeds, sometimes on the ground but is nimble enough to hang on to thistles and teasels in the wind. Quite a slender beak for a finch. Has an attractive jingling metallic call, which led to the collective noun, a 'charm' of goldfinches.

Siskin

Carduelis spinus

A small finch, which breeds in small numbers but visits Cornwall mostly in the winter to feed in waterside alders and pines. The male (right) has a green and yellow plumage with a black forehead and chin. Females (left) and juveniles are browner, with heavy streaking. Always occurs in flocks during the winter, and is usually twittering as it feeds. Breeds mostly to the east of the county in plantations around Bodmin Moor.

Linnet

Carduelis cannabina

A common bird of farmland and coast. The male (left) in breeding plumage has a ginger back, red breast and red forehead. Females (right), juveniles and males out of season are less colourful but always show a flash of white in the wing. Found most commonly around the coast where gorse grows, it is here that they nest. Its song is attractive, and this is why they were once kept as cage birds.

Bullfinch

Pyrrhula pyrrhula

The male (left) bullfinch is a striking bird with scarlet red breast, white rump, grey back, black wings and a black cap. Females (right) are similar in pattern, but have a brown body and back. Juveniles are like females, but also have a brown head. Quite shy birds, but often located by their constant, gentle 'few-few' calls. Will eat buds and blossom in the spring. Always found along hedgerows and woodland edges. Widespread across the county though never numerous.

J	F	M	A	M	J	J	A	S	O	N	D

Yellowhammer
Emberiza citrinella

This is a large bunting, bigger than a chaffinch. The male yellowhammer (above) has a bright yellow face and ginger back. The female (right) has some yellow in her plumage, but is browner and more heavily streaked. The male has a characteristic song – 'a-little-bit-of-bread-and-no-cheeeeese', which it makes from the tops of bushes in hedgerows. This is a bird of farmland, but will also occupy gorse bushes where they grow close to arable fields. Quite a long-tailed bird when seen in flight. Feeds mostly on the ground.

| J | F | M | A | M | J | J | A | S | O | N | D |

often found breeding near reedbeds, but not exclusively. Regularly found feeding on farmland, and sometimes roosts in large numbers on heath and moorland. Has a distinctive 'tseeu' call. Breeds in the county but is more numerous in winter

Reed Bunting
Emberiza schoeniclus

The male reed bunting (right) has a distinctive black head pattern with white collar and moustache. The female (left) has a similar patterning but is brown rather than black. Both have a longish tail with white edges. It is

Corn Bunting
Miliaria calandra

A large, chunky bunting associated with arable farming. Basically brown but heavily streaked, paler underneath than on top, a little like a skylark. In spring it regularly sings from fence-posts, bushes and wires. Its song is easily identifiable and sounds like a bunch of jangling keys. This bird is only found on the north coast of Cornwall, and its distribution is very much centred on Trevose Head.

J F M A M J J A S O N D

Some Top Spots for Birding

Annet, SV 86 08, IOS, island (puffins, shearwaters), only accessed by boat trip from St Mary's, 8, 43

Boscastle, SX 09 91, Boscastle, coast (razorbills, guillemots)

Bude Canal and marshes, SS 20 05, Bude, wetland (wildfowl, waders)

Cabilla and Redrice Woods, SX 128 653, Bodmin, woodland, CWT reserve, access for all, 66

Camel Estuary, SW 93 74, Wadebridge, estuary (waders, wildfowl), 12, 28

Cape Cornwall, SW 35 31, St Just, headland (seabirds)

Cardinham Woods, SX 100 667, Bodmin, woods (mixed), FE, parking charge

Cargreen, SX 43 62, Saltash, estuary (waders, wildfowl), 27

Carnsew Pool, SW 55 37, Hayle, tidal lake (great northern diver), RSPB reserve, access for all, 6

Carrick Roads, SW 83 35, Falmouth, coastal inlet, 18

Church Cove, Lizard, SW 715 127, Lizard, valley (migrants)

Colliford Lake, SX 17 72, Bodmin, reservoir (gulls, wildfowl), 7, 12

Copperhouse Creek, SW 56 37, Hayle, estuary (wildfowl, waders), RSPB, free access

Cot Valley, SW 36 30, St Just, valley (migrants), NT

Cotehele, SX 424 682, Callington, woodland, estuary, NT, 71

Crowdy Reservoir, SX 14 83, Camelford, reservoir (gulls,

wildfowl), SWLT, access for all, 12, 77

Davidstow Airfield, SX 14 85, Camelford, disused airfield (waders)

Drift Reservoir, SW 437 288, Penzance, reservoir (gulls, wildfowl), CBWPS, access by permit, 12, 14

Gannel Estuary, SW 79 61, Newquay, estuary (wildfowl, waders)

Garrison, The, SV 89 10, IOS, St Mary's, headland (migrants, seabirds)

Gerrans Bay, SW 90 37, St Mawes, coastal (divers, grebes)

Godrevy, SW 582 432, Hayle, headland (migrants, seabirds), NT, 4, 31

Golitha Falls, SX 228 689,

Index of Birds Recorded Annually

This index lists birds likely to be recorded annually in Cornwall and the Isles of Scilly. Species are listed alphabetically by common name, followed by scientific name, status, calendar, typical habitat, best locations, and page number in the book. Entries in green type denote species that have photographs.

Key to status:
- CO – common: likely to be seen if visiting the correct habitat at the correct time of year
- UC – uncommon: only present in small numbers

- RA – rare: recorded annually, but only likely to be seen with a special effort
- VR – very rare: probably recorded annually, but unlikely to be seen

Key to calendar:
- R – resident
- W – winter visitor
- aut – autumn migrant
- spr – spring migrant
- sum – summer visitor

Note: months also abbreviated

R, woodland and garden, 79

Chiffchaff, *Phylloscopus collybita*, CO, R, woodland and scrub, 65

Chough, *Pyrrhocorax pyrrhocorax* , RA, R, coastal heath and cliffs, The Lizard Point and Land's End, 74

Coot, *Fulica atra*, CO, R, ponds and lakes, 25

Cormorant, *Phalacrocorax carbo*, CO, R, inland waterways and coast, 10

Crake, spotted, *Porzana porzana*, VR, aug, sep, wetland, Marazion

Crossbill, *Loxia curvirostra*, VR, spr, aut, woodland (pine)

Crow, carrion, *Corvus corone*, CO, R, farmland and coast, 76

Cuckoo, *Cuculus canorus*, UC, sum, heathland, 45

Curlew, *Numenius arquata*, CO, R commoner in W, estuary, 33

D

Dipper, *Cinclus cinclus*, CO, R, rivers, 54

Diver, black-throated, *Gavia arctica*, RA, W, sea, Gerrans Bay, St Austell Bay, 6

Diver, great northern, *Gavia immer*, UC, W, sea, Carnsew Pool, 6

Diver, red-throated, *Gavia stellata*, VR, W, sea, Whitsand Bay, 6

Dotterel, *Charadrius morinellus*, VR, spr, aut, hills and estuary, Davidstow airfield

Dove, collared, *Streptopelia decaocto*, CO, R, farmland and garden, 45

Dove, rock (feral pigeon), *Columba livia*, CO, R, coastal cliffs, 44

Dove, stock, *Columba oenas*, UC, R, woodland and farmland, 44

Dove, turtle, *Streptopelia turtur*, RA, spr, aut, woodland and farmland

Duck, long-tailed, *Clangula hyemalis*, VR, W, sea

Duck, ruddy, *Oxyura jamaicensis*, RA, W, lakes

Duck, tufted, *Aythya fuligula*, CO, R commoner in W, lakes, 17

Dunlin, *Calidris alpina*, CO, W, estuary and beaches, 31

Dunnock, *Prunella modularis*, CO, R, woodland, hedgerow and garden, 55

E

Egret, little, *Egretta garzetta*, CO, R, estuary, 11

Eider, *Somateria mollissima*, VR, W, sea

F

Falcon, peregrine, *Falco peregrinus*, UC, R, coastal cliffs, 21

Fieldfare, *Turdus pilaris*, CO, W, farmland, 60

Firecrest, *Regulus ignicapilla*, VR, aut and W, woodland, 66

Flycatcher, pied, *Ficedula hypoleuca*, UC, sum, woodland (deciduous), Valleys of West Penwith and Isles of Scilly, on migration, 66

Flycatcher, red-breasted, *Ficedula parva*, VR, aut, coastal scrub, Valleys of West Penwith and Isles of Scilly, on migration

Flycatcher, spotted, *Muscicapa striata*, CO, sum, woodland, woodland of east Cornwall, 67

Fulmar, *Fulmarus glacialis*, CO, R, coastal cliffs, 8

G

Gadwall, *Anas strepera*, CO, W, lakes, 14

Gannet, *Morus bassanus*, CO, All year, sea, 9

Garganey, *Anas querquedula*, VR, spr, lake, Marazion

Godwit, bar-tailed, *Limosa lapponica*, UC, W, estuary, Camel Estuary, 32

Godwit, black-tailed, *Limosa*

limosa, CO, W, estuary, Fal Estuary, 32

Goldcrest, *Regulus regulus*, CO, R, woodland, 66

Goldeneye, *Bucephala clangula*, UC, W, lakes and estuary, Carrick Roads, Loe Pool, 18

Goldfinch, *Carduelis carduelis*, CO, R, scrub and garden, 80

Goosander, *Mergus merganser*, UC, W, lakes and estuary, 19

Goose, barnacle, *Branta leucopsis*, VR, W, lake and estuary

Goose, brent, *Branta bernicla*, VR, W, lake and estuary

Goose, Canada, *Branta canadensis*, CO, R, lakes, ponds and estuary, Colliford and Crowdy reservoirs, 12

Goose, European white-fronted, *Anser albifrons albifrons*, VR, W, lake and estuary

Goose, pink-footed, *Anser brachyrhynchus*, VR, W, lake and estuary

Goose, greylag, *Anser anser*, UC, W, lakes and estuary

Grebe, black-necked, *Podiceps nigricollis*, VR, W, sea and estuary, Carrick Roads, Gerrans Bay

Grebe, great crested, *Podiceps cristatus*, UC, R commoner in W, lakes, Tamar Lakes, Lynher Estuary, St Austell Bay, 7

Grebe, little, *Tachybaptus ruficollis*, CO, R commoner in W, areas of still fresh water, 7

Grebe, red-necked, *Podiceps grisegena*, VR, W, sea and estuary

Grebe, Slavonian, *Podiceps auritus*, VR, W, sea and estuary, Carrick Roads, Gerrans Bay

Greenfinch, *Carduelis chloris*, CO, R, woodland and garden, 80

Greenshank, *Tringa nebularia*, CO, W, estuary, 34

Guillemot, *Uria aalge*, CO, R, rocky islands, Isles of Scilly and islands near Boscastle, 42

Guillemot, black, *Cepphus grylle*, VR, W, sea

Gull, black-headed, *Larus ridibundus*, CO, W, farm fields, lakes and coastal, 36

Gull, Bonaparte's, *Larus philadelphia*, VR, aut, sea, coastal headlands of Penwith

Gull, common, *Larus canus*, CO, W, farm fields, lakes and coastal, 37

Gull, glaucous, *Larus hyperboreus*, VR, W, harbours and estuary

Gull, great black-backed, *Larus marinus*, CO, R, coast, 39

Gull, herring, *Larus argentatus argenteus*, CO, R, coast, reservoirs and farm fields, 38

Gull, Iceland, *Larus glaucoides*, VR, W, reservoirs, harbours and estuary

Gull, lesser black-backed, *Larus fuscus*, CO, R, coast, 37

Gull, little, *Larus minutus*, VR, W, coastal and lakes

Gull, Mediterranean, *Larus melanocephalus*, RA, W, coastal, Camel Estuary and Millbrook

Gull, ring-billed, *Larus delawarensis*, VR, W, coastal and estuary

Gull, Sabine's, *Larus sabini*, VR, aut, sea, coastal headlands of Penwith

Gull, yellow-legged, *Larus argentatus michahellis*, VR, W, coastal and estuary

H

Harrier, hen, *Circus cyaneus*, RA, migrant and W, moorland

Harrier, marsh, *Circus aeruginosus*, RA, spr, aut, wetland, breeds on Tresco

Harrier, Montagu's, *Circus pygargus*, VR, spr, aut, wet-land, heathland and farmland

Heron, grey, *Ardea cinerea*, CO, R, any area of water, 11

Heron, purple, *Ardea purpurea*, VR, spr, wetland

Hobby, *Falco subbuteo*, RA, R but commoner in spr and aut, wetland

Hoopoe, *Upupa epops*, VR, spr, aut, short grassland, coastal valleys of West Penwith

J

Jackdaw, *Corvus monedula*, CO, R, woodland and coastal cliff, 75

Jay, *Garrulus glandarius*, CO, R, woodland, 73

K

Kestrel, *Falco tinnunculus*, CO, R, rough grassland, 21

Kingfisher, *Alcedo atthis*, UC, R, rivers and estuary, 47

Kite, red, *Milvus milvus*, VR, spr, farmland and woodland, coastal headlands

Kittiwake, *Rissa tridactyla*, CO, R, coastal cliffs, 40

Knot, *Calidris canutus*, UC, W, estuary, Camel Estuary, 30

L

Lapwing, *Vanellus vanellus*, CO, R commoner in W, estuary and farm fields, Camel and Hayle Estuary, 29

Lark, short-toed, *Calandrella brachydactyla*, VR, aut, grassland on coast, coastal headlands of Penwith

Linnet, *Carduelis cannabina*, CO, R, heathland, 81

M

Magpie, *Pica pica*, CO, R, woodland and farmland, 73

Mallard, *Anas platyrhynchos*, CO, R, any areas of water, 15

Martin, house, *Delichon urbica*, CO, sum, nesting on houses, 51

Martin, sand, *Riparia riparia*, CO, sum, coastal sandy cliffs, 50

Merganser, red-breasted, *Mergus serrator*, UC, W, lakes and estuary, Carrick Roads, Millbrook, 18

Merlin, *Falco columbarius*, RA, W, moorland and coast

Moorhen, *Gallinula chloropus*, CO, R, any areas of water or marsh, 24

N

Nightjar, *Caprimulgus europaeus*, VR, sum, heath-land, Goonhilly and Goss Moor

Nuthatch, *Sitta europaea*, CO, R, woodland and garden, 71

O

Oriole, golden, *Oriolus oriolus*, VR, spr, any, Valleys of West Penwith and Isles of Scilly, on

migration

Osprey, *Pandion haliaetus*, VR, spr, aut, estuary and lakes, Camel, Hayle and Fal Estuary

Owl, barn, *Tyto alba*, UC, R, farmland, 46

Owl, little, *Athene noctua*, VR, R, moors, farmland and coastal

Owl, long-eared, *Asio otus*, VR, W, woodland

Owl, short-eared, *Asio flammeus*, VR, W, moorland, Moors of Penwith

Owl, tawny, *Strix aluco*, CO, R, woodland, 46

Oystercatcher, *Haematopus ostralegus*, CO, R commoner in W, rocky coasts in summer, estuary in winter, 26

P

Partridge, grey, *Perdix perdix*, RA, R, farmland, 22

Partridge, red-legged, *Alectoris rufa*, UC, R, farmland, 22

Petrel, Leach's, *Oceanodroma leucorhoa*, VR, Sep to Nov, sea, Headlands of Penwith

Petrel, storm, *Hydrobates pelagicus*, VR, sum, sea, Headlands of Penwith

Phalarope, grey, *Phalaropus fulicarius*, VR, migrant and W, coastal and lakes, coastal headlands of Penwith

Pheasant, *Phasianus colchicus*, CO, R, woodland, farmland and garden, 23

Pigeon, feral, see Dove, rock

Pigeon, wood, *Columba palumbus*, CO, R, woodland and farmland, 44

Pintail, *Anas acuta*, UC, W, lakes and estuary, 15

Pipit, meadow, *Anthus pratensis*, CO, R, coarse grassland and heath, 52

Pipit, Richard's, *Anthus novaeseelandiae*, VR, aut, grassland on coast, coastal headlands of Penwith

Pipit, rock, *Anthus petrosus*, CO, R, coastal, 52

Pipit, tawny, *Anthus campestris*, VR, aut, grassland on coast, coastal headlands of Penwith

Pipit, tree, *Anthus. trivialis*, UC, sum, clearings in managed coniferous woodland, around Bodmin Moor

Pipit, water, *Anthus spinoletta*, VR, W, wet grassland

Plover, American golden, *Pluvialis dominica*, VR, spr, aut, farmland and estuary, Davidstow airfield

Plover, golden, *Pluvialis apricaria*, CO, W, estuary and farm fields, Crowdy and Colliford, 28

Plover, grey, *Pluvialis squatarola*, CO, W, estuary and rocky coasts, Hayle Estuary, 28

Plover, Kentish, *Charadrius alexandrinus*, VR, spr, aut, estuary, Hayle Estuary

Plover, little-ringed, *Charadrius dubius*, VR, spr, aut, wetland

Plover, ringed, *Charadrius hiaticula*, CO, mostly W, R on Scilly, sandy and pebble beaches, 27

Pochard, *Aythya ferina*, CO, W, lakes, Loe Pool, 16

Puffin, *Fratercula arctica*, UC, R, islands, Isles of Scilly and The Mouls, 43

Q

Quail, *Coturnix coturnix*, VR, sum, farmland

R

Rail, water, *Rallus aquaticus*, UC, W, wetland, Marazion, Swanpool, 24

Raven, *Corvus corax*, CO, R, mostly coastal but also woodland, 76

Razorbill, *Alca torda*, CO, R, rocky islands, Isles of Scilly and islands near Boscastle, 42

Redpoll, lesser, *Carduelis cabaret*, VR, R, woodland

Redshank, *Tringa totanus*, CO, W, estuary, 34

Redshank, spotted, *Tringa erythropus*, UC, W, estuary, Tresillian River, 34

Redstart, *Phoenicurus phoenicurus*, UC, sum, woodland (deciduous), breeding around edge of Bodmin Moor, 56

Redstart, black, *Phoenicurus ochruros*, RA, aut, beaches and buildings, Isles of Scilly, 56

Redwing, *Turdus iliacus*, CO, W, farmland, 61

Ring Ouzel, *Turdus torquatus*, VR, spr, aut, hills and coast, Headlands of Penwith

Robin, *Erithacus rubecula*, CO, R, garden, 55

Rook, *Corvus frugilegus*, CO, R, woodland and farmland, 75

Ruff, *Philomachus pugnax*, UC, W, estuary

S

Sanderling, *Calidris alba*, CO, W, sandy beaches, Mounts Bay, 30

Sandpiper, buff-breasted, *Tryngites subruficollis*, VR, aut, estuary, Davidstow airfield

Sandpiper, common, *Actitis hypoleucos*, UC, spr, aut, estuary and lakes, Hayle Estuary, 35

Sandpiper, curlew, *Calidris ferruginea*, RA, Sep, Oct, estuary, Hayle and Camel

Estuary

Sandpiper, green, *Tringa ochropus*, RA, Jul to Sep, margins of pools and lakes, Stithians Reservoir

Sandpiper, pectoral, *Calidris melanotos*, VR, aut, estuary and lakes

Sandpiper, purple, *Calidris maritima*, UC, W, rocky beaches, Jubilee Pool, Penzance, 31

Sandpiper, wood, *Tringa glareola*, RA, Jul to Sep, margins of pools and lakes, Stithians Reservoir

Scaup, *Aythya marila*, RA, W, lakes and sea, Loe Pool, Drift Reservoir, 17

Scoter, common, *Melanitta nigra*, UC, W, sea, 17

Scoter, velvet, *Melanitta fusca*, VR, W, sea

Serin, *Serinus serinus*, VR, spr, aut, woodland and coastal, Valleys of West Penwith and Isles of Scilly, on migration

Shag, *Phalacrocorax aristotelis*, CO, R, rocky coasts, 10

Shearwater, Balearic, *Puffinus mauretanicus*, VR, Jul to Oct, sea, Headlands of Penwith

Shearwater, Cory's, *Calonectris diomedea*, RA, Jul to Sep, sea, Headlands of Penwith

Shearwater, great, *Puffinus gravis*, RA, Jul to Sep, sea, Headlands of Penwith

Shearwater, Manx, *Puffinus puffinus*, UC, Mar to Oct, sea and islands, Headlands of Penwith, 8

Shearwater, sooty, *Puffinus griseus*, VR, Jul to Oct, sea, Headlands of Penwith

Shelduck, *Tadorna tadorna*, CO, R, estuary, 13

Shoveler, *Anas clypeata*, UC, W, lakes, Loe Pool, 16

Shrike, great grey, *Lanius excubitor*, VR, W, heathland, Goonhilly and Goss Moor

Shrike, red-backed, *Lanius collurio*, VR, spr, aut, coastal heath, Valleys of West Penwith and Isles of Scilly, on migration

Shrike, woodchat, *Lanius senator*, VR, spr, coastal heath, Valleys of West Penwith and Isles of Scilly, on migration

Siskin, *Carduelis spinus*, UC, R, damp woodland, 81

Skua, Arctic, *Stercorarius parasiticus*, RA, aut, sea, coastal headlands of Penwith

Skua, great, *Catharacta skua*, RA, aut, sea, coastal head-lands of Penwith

Skua, long-tailed, *Stercorarius longicaudus*, VR, aut, sea, coastal headlands of Penwith

Skua, pomarine, *Stercorarius pomarinus*, VR, aut, sea, coastal headlands of Penwith

Skylark, *Alauda arvensis*, CO, R, farmland and dunes, 50

Smew, *Mergus albellus*, VR, W, lake

Snipe, *Gallinago gallinago*, CO, R commoner in W, marshy land, 32

Snipe, jack, *Lymnocryptes minimus*, VR, W, wetland, Lower Moors, St Mary's

Sparrow, house, *Passer domesticus*, CO, R, garden and farmland, 78

Sparrow, tree, *Passer montanus*, VR, spr, aut, farmland, 78

Sparrowhawk, *Accipiter nisus*, CO, R, woodland, farmland and garden, 20

Spoonbill, *Platalea leucorodia*, VR, W, estuary, Lynher Estuary

Starling, *Sturnus vulgaris*, CO, R, towns and farmland, 77

Starling, rose-coloured, *Sturnus roseus*, VR, aut, farmland, Valleys of West Penwith and Isles of Scilly, on migration

Stint, little, *Calidris minuta*, VR, Sep, Oct, estuary, Hayle Estuary

Stonechat, *Saxicola torquata*, CO, R, heaths, 57

Swallow, *Hirundo rustica*, CO,

bed, 63

Warbler, sedge, *Acrocephalus schoenabaenus*, CO, sum, reedbed, 62

Warbler, willow, *Phylloscopus trochilus*, CO, sum, woodland and scrub, 65

Warbler, wood, *Phylloscopus sibilatrix*, RA, sum, woodland (deciduous), mature woodlands of East Cornwall

Warbler, yellow-browed, *Phylloscopus inornatus*, VR, aut, scrub and woodland, Valleys of West Penwith and Isles of Scilly, on migration

Waxwing, *Bombycilla garrulus*, VR, W, around berry bearing bushes

Wheatear, *Oenanthe oenanthe*, CO, sum, coastal and moorland, 57

Whimbrel, *Numenius phaeopus*, UC, migrant, mostly April and May, estuary and beaches, 33

Whinchat, *Saxicola rubetra*, UC, sum, moorland, breeding around Bodmin Moor

Whitethroat, *Sylvia communis*, CO, sum, heathland, 64

Whitethroat, lesser, *Sylvia curruca*, VR, sum, heaths and coast, Valleys of West Penwith and Isles of Scilly, on migration

Wigeon, *Anas penelope*, CO, W, estuary and lakes, Hayle Estuary, 13

Wigeon, American, *Anas americana*, VR, W, estuary, Hayle Estuary

Woodcock, *Scolopax rusticola*, UC, W, damp woodland

Woodlark, *Lullula arborea*, VR, W, farmland

Woodpecker, great spotted, *Dendrocopos major*, CO, R, woodland and garden, 49

Woodpecker, green, *Picus viridis*, CO, R, woodland and coastal grassland, 48

Woodpecker, lesser spotted, *Dendrocopos minor*, VR, R, woodland, mature woodlands of East Cornwall, 49

Wren, *Troglodytes troglodytes*, CO, R, woodland and garden, 54

Wryneck, *Jynx torquilla*, VR, spr, aut, any, usually near coast, coastal valleys of West Penwith

Y

Yellowhammer, *Emberiza citrinella*, CO, R, farmland, 83

Organizations and Groups

Cornwall Birds (previously The Cornwall
Bird-Watching & Preservation Society)
membership secretary is Sara McMahon
Tel: 01752 242 823
Email at sara@surfbirder.com

**Cornwall County Council,
Environment & Heritage Section**
Cornwall County Council, Old County Hall,
Truro TR1 3AY
Tel: 01872 222 **000**
www.cornwall.gov.uk

Cornwall Wildlife Trust
Five Acres, Allet, nr Truro TR4 9DJ
Tel: 01872 273 939
www.cornwallwildlifetrust.org.uk

Isles of Scilly Wildlife Trust
Carn Thomas, St Mary's,
Isles of Scilly TR21 0PT
Tel: 01720 422 153
www.ios-wildlifetrust.org.uk

National Trust, Cornwall Office
Lanhydrock, Bodmin PL30 4DE
Tel: 01208 742 81
www.nationaltrust.org.uk

**Natural England, Cornwall &
Isles of Scilly Team**
Trevint House, Strangways Villas,
Truro TR1 2PA
Tel: 01872 265 710,
head office 01733 455 **000**
www.naturalengland.org.uk

Royal Society for the Protection of Birds
The RSPB South West Regional Office,
Keble House, Southernhay Gardens,
Exeter EX1 1NT
Tel: 01392 432 691
www.rspb.org.uk